How Many Hours?

by Katherine Krieg

Say Hello to Amicus Readers.

You'll find our helpful dog, Amicus, chasing a ball—to let you know the reading level of a book.

1

Learn to Read

Frequent repetition, high frequency words, and close photo-text matches introduce familiar topics and provide ample support for brand new readers.

2

Read Independently

Some repetition is mixed with varied sentence structures and a select amount of new vocabulary words are introduced with text and photo support.

3

Read to Know More

Interesting facts and engaging art and photos give fluent readers fun books both for reading practice and to learn about new topics.

Amicus Readers are published by Amicus
P.O. Box 1329, Mankato, MN 56002
www.amicuspublishing.us

Photo Credits: iStock/Thinkstock, cover; Michael Jung/Shutterstock Images, 1; Dejan Ristovski/ Shutterstock Images, 3; Lucian Coman/ Shutterstock Images, 4–5; iStockphoto, 7, 11; Bernd Juergens/Shutterstock Images, 8; Shutterstock Images, 12, 14–15, 16 (bottom); Matthew Benoit/ Shutterstock Images, 13; William Casey/ Shutterstock Images, 16 (top)

Produced for Amicus by The Peterson Publishing Company and Red Line Editorial.

Editor Jenna Gleisner
Designer Becky Daum

Oct15 J

Library of Congress
Cataloging-in-Publication Data
Krieg, Katherine, author.
  How many hours? / by Katherine Krieg.
    pages cm. -- (Amicus readers level 2)
(Measuring time)
  Summary: "Introduces activities young readers experience in a matter of hours, such as cooking a meal or watching a movie, while teaching ways to measure an hour and how it compares to minutes and days."-- Provided by publisher.
  Audience: K to grade 3
  ISBN 978-1-60753-722-9 (library binding)
  ISBN 978-1-60753-826-4 (ebook)
  1. Time--Juvenile literature. 2. Time measurements--Juvenile literature. I. Title.
  QB209.5.K746 2014
  529.7--dc23
                                      2014049949

Printed in Malaysia
10 9 8 7 6 5 4 3 2 1

We use hours to measure time. There are 60 minutes in 1 hour. We do not have school today. What can we do in a few hours at home?

Shay helps her mom water
the garden. It takes her
1 hour
to water all of the flowers.

Chase and his dad make lasagna. They set the timer for **1 hour.** They will eat the lasagna for lunch.

COOK TIME

TIMED OVEN

COOK TIME | DELAY START TIME | STOP TIME

They save some lasagna for Chase's mom. She is at work for **8 hours.** She will be home when the clock reads 5:00.

After lunch, Liz and her brother watch their favorite movie. The movie lasts **2 hours.**

It is 3:00. Tomorrow at 3:00, Liz will be coming home from school. That is **24 hours** from now, or 1 full day.

There are many things to do in 1 hour.

What can you do in 1 hour at home?

Measuring Hours

hour hand

second hand

minute hand

hours

minutes

HOUR

MIN

START/ STOP

RESET

1:00